Lying as Still as I Can

Barry Behrstock

Illustrated by JoAnn Adinolfi

Rigby

© 1999 by Rigby
a division of Reed Elsevier Inc.
500 Coventry Lane
Crystal Lake, IL 60014

Executive Editor: Lynelle H. Morgenthaler
Senior Designer: Tom Sjoerdsma

04 03 02 01 00
10 9 8 7 6 5 4

Printed in Singapore

ISBN 0-7635-5714-5

One night my mom said, "It's time for bed, Jason. Now lie still and go to sleep."

But then I thought . . .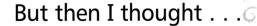

How can I really lie *still* when I'm on a boat that is moving up and down and traveling across the ocean?

And how can I lie still when the ocean is moving? It is part of our Earth, which is spinning like a top, making one turn each day.

So I'm *trying* to lie still, BUT
I'm on a boat that is moving
on the Earth that is spinning.

Our Earth is part of the solar system, a group of nine planets and the sun.

The Earth, like all of the planets, is not just spinning. It is also circling the sun like a ball swinging by a string around a pole.

So I'm *trying* to lie still, BUT
    I'm on a boat that is moving
        on the Earth that is spinning
          and circling around the sun.

Our sun and billions of other suns are part of the Milky Way Galaxy. From Earth the Milky Way Galaxy looks like a river of stars across a dark night sky.

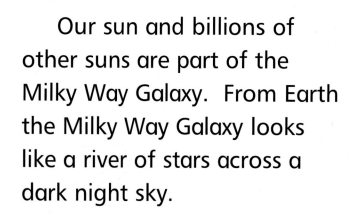

And the Milky Way Galaxy is not standing still. It is slowly turning in space like a giant pinwheel.

So I'm *trying* to lie still, BUT
   I'm on a boat that is moving
      on the Earth that is spinning
         and circling around the sun
            in a slowly turning galaxy.

Our Milky Way Galaxy and billions and
billions of other galaxies are part of the universe.
All of these galaxies are turning slowly.

As the galaxies turn, they are also moving outward in space like dots spreading apart when you blow up a balloon. So the universe is getting bigger and bigger!

So I'm moving in a giant universe that's getting even bigger . . .

in a galaxy that is turning . . .

on the Earth, which is circling around the sun
and spinning once each day, . . .

on a boat that is moving . . .

while I'm in my bed,
LYING AS STILL AS I CAN!